D0605559

Can I TOUCH Your Hair?

Poems of Race, Mistakes, and Friendship

Irene Latham & Charles Waters

Illustrated by Sean Qualls & Selina Alko

Carolrhoda Books · Minneapolis

"Salvation for a race, nation, or class
must come from within."
—A. Philip Randolph

"The only thing that will redeem
mankind is cooperation."
—Bertrand Russell

CONTENTS

The Poem Project

When our teacher says,
Pick a partner,
my body freezes
like a ship in ice.

I want Patty Jean,
but Madison
has already looped
arms with her.

Within seconds,
you-never-know-what-
he's-going-to-say Charles
is the only one left.

How many poems?
someone asks.
About what?
Do they have to be true?

Mrs. Vandenberg
holds up her hand.
Write about anything!
It's not black and white.

But it is.
Charles is black,
and I'm white.

WRITING PARTNER

Mrs. Vandenberg wants us to write poems?
Finally, an easy project. Words fly off my pen
onto the paper, like writing is my superpower.
The rest of the time, my words are a curse. I open my mouth,
and people run away. Now I'm stuck with Irene?
She hardly says anything. Plus she's white.
Her stringy, dishwater blond hair waves
back and forth as she stutter-steps toward me.
My stomach bottoms out. "Hello," I say. "Hi," she says.
I surprise myself by smiling at her—she smells like
a mix of perfume and soap. We stare at our sneakers
before I ask, "So, what do you want to
write about?" She shrugs. I say, "How about our shoes, hair?
Then we can write about school and church?"
She takes a deep breath. "Okay."
I match it. "Let's start there."

Shoes

I want ruby shoes
with heels to click
me to another land

or glass slippers
to make a dancer
out of me.

But Mama says
shoes should be
sensible—

plain white
or solid black
to go with everything.

So that's what we buy.
When I show Patty Jean,
she gives me

her rainbow socks
and a pair of purple
shoelaces.

When I look down,
I can't believe
those feet belong to me.

SHOPPING WITH DAD

Dad doesn't think shoes have anything to do with
fashion. "Shoes are like your complexion," he says.
"They're supposed to fit you perfectly."
I'd rather get another pair of neon high-tops
with tie-dye laces, like I've seen on commercials.
Maybe they make my feet hurt sometimes,
and maybe they don't last as long,
but at least I fit in with my classmates.
Dad hands me a pair of low tops,
no cool design, no bright color or dynamite laces.
I tie them up, walk around. "Wow," I say.
"This pair feels like I'm wearing slippers."
Dad tells me, "The decision is yours."

Hair

Now my hair
is long and straight—
a curtain I can hide
behind.

But once,
when I was little,
I begged
for an Afro.

So Mama cut
my hair short
as a boy's
and gave me a perm.

I fluffed it
with a pick
big as
it would go—

until my brothers
laughed,
called me
a circus clown

without the red nose.

STRANDS

On a random Tuesday on the bus,
Dennis asks me, "Can I touch your hair?" He pats it
before I can respond. "It feels like a sponge," he says.
My fists clench, and my face gets hot. "You need to learn to wait
for an answer after asking permission," I tell him and pat his hair, *hard*.
"Oh, how about that? Your hair feels like a mop." I say.
I keep my fists ready, but he turns away.

Church

At church
we light candles
and pray for those
who are sick.

At church
we *sit stand kneel*.
We give thanks
for food and warmth
and family.

At church
the sun streams through
our stained-glass Jesus,
his arms thrown wide
to welcome
everyone.

At church
everyone is white.

SUNDAY SERVICE

Our Sunday service is like hitting a reset button,
starting off the week with a new beginning.
There's men dressed in suits so sharp you could cut
yourself by looking at them, there's women testifying
in wide-brimmed, bow-tied hats called *crowns*.
Everyone's brown arms are raised in devotion,
except mine. If it says in the Bible that Jesus
had hair like wool, eyes that were a flame of fire,
and feet like brass as if they burned in a furnace,
then why is everyone praising the straight-haired,
blue-eyed white man I see looking down over all of us?

BEACH DAY

There's a pack of guys and girls, whose pearly skins
have been baked into a bronzed hue, strolling past me.
Each of them has hair woven into cornrows
or twisted into dreadlocks.
Some of their lips jut out like puffer fish.
When I wave, they look at each other, begin snorting,
laughing at my good manners.
I feel a fury rising inside me, as if I'm a
tidal wave about to crash on land.
I'm confused: why do people who
want to look like me hate me so much?

Beach

While the older girls
shine themselves
with cooking oil
to get the perfect
flapjack tan,

Mama makes
a ghost of me.

She slathers on
sunscreen so thick
I turn stiff and sticky
and my eyes sting.

When Mama's
not looking,
I scrub it all off
with a towel.

I'd rather be
sunburned
than sugar-sand white.

THE ATHLETE

In gym class, when captains select teammates
for a game of basketball, I get picked first,
maybe for being lanky or for having darker skin.
I guess it seems like a good idea to them, until
I take a shot that goes over the backboard.
I get picked last for basketball after that.

During reading time when Mrs. Vandenberg says
we each have to read a chapter of
The Watsons Go to Birmingham—1963,
everyone groans when it's my turn,
until the words gush out of my mouth,
smooth and fast like the River Jordan.
By the time I'm done, smiles spread
across each classmate's face.
I now get selected to read first every time.

in the air
once, it took for

ONE OF THOSE DAYS THAT...

YOUR BREATH
KIND OF HUNG FROZEN
iN THE
AIR...

Horseback Riding

I don't know how to explain
to Charles how I feel about horses
when he shuffles so fast
from one subject to the next.

Finally, I blurt, *sometimes I just need*
a break from people.

He surprises me and shuts up right away,
so I tell him about the sweet scent
of hay and saddle soap,
how my stomach somersaults

when Honey surges from trot to canter,
and how the wind parts my hair
when I lean into her neck,
whispering, *faster, faster.*

When I want Honey to slow down,
all I have to do
is give the reins a gentle tug,
and soon we are back to *clop-clopping.*

Honey and I understand each other
without any words at all.

Playground

After lunch
I skip past the swings
and basketball court
to the spot by the fence
where the black girls
play freeze dance.

I watch for a few minutes,
hoping Shonda
will invite me to join them
instead of me having to ask,
can I play?

I smile when Shonda
comes over, but she doesn't
smile back. *You've got
the whole rest of the playground,*
she says. *Can't we
at least have this corner?*

FRESH START

Some kids huddle together by the swings
gabbing about the football game when I spot J.R. and Nicholas.
They're the only two friends who came by last summer
when I invited everyone to swim in our pool.
When I walk over, J.R. says, "C'mon, man, stay away
from us." Nicholas breaks in, "Your mouth is like a race car
that never stops to refuel." The group shakes with laughter,
I can't believe my "friends" would play me dirty like that.
My body crumples before I mope over to Irene,
who's watching some girls play freeze dance.
I plop down next to her. "Want to work on our project?"

GHOST

There's a new student at school who I haven't met yet.
He goes by the name Ghost, at least that's what his new
friends, all the same color, call him.
I introduce myself, "Hey, Ghost, my name's Charles."
His pasty skin heats up faster than a summer's day.
"My name's Paul," he says, leaving my outstretched
hand to dangle. I realize I'm a few shades too dark
to be allowed to call him by his nickname.

Geography

When Mrs. Vandenberg
points at the US map
and asks, *Why do we call
this region the black belt?*
I stretch my hand high.
But she calls on Patty Jean
instead.

Patty Jean leans forward,
like she's sure she's right.
Because black people live there.
Mrs. Vandenberg's face
squinches like a rotten peach,
and her voice comes out sour.
Of course not, Patty Jean.
Use your head.

I sink down into my seat.
Patty Jean's answer is my answer.
I learn
when it comes to black and white,
sometimes it's best
to press my lips closed
and not say anything at all.

DINNER CONVERSATION

Grandma and Grandpa are visiting, so our
dining room table is filled with soul food:
crispy fried chicken coated in seasoning,
gooey, creamy, baked macaroni and cheese,
collard greens mixed with chunks of ham hock,
red velvet cake smeared in cream cheese icing.
But I can't eat any of this. A few weeks ago I
became a vegan, which means no meat or dairy foods for me.
Mom brings out my plate filled with beans, rice, and
pumpkin, I sprinkle Himalayan sea salt and chili pepper on top.
"I don't understand this." Dad says, "Soul food is our history."
I clamp my teeth down to hold back everything
I want to say about how soul food leads to cancer and diabetes.
How unfair that trillions of animals get killed every year for food and clothing!
Instead, I swallow hard and say nothing.
Everybody gazes at the food, silent. Dad shakes his head.
Grandma turns away from the family,
smiles, then gives me a wink
as we begin to say grace.

Best and Worst

Each night we go around
the supper table, say
the best part of our day
and the worst.
Bests are easy
as creamed potatoes:
an A on my math test,
Pajama Day, new shoes.
Worsts stick in my throat
like tiny fish bones:
the bracelet I lost and still
can't find, my sniffly nose,
what Shonda said at recess.
But saying it out loud helps.
We listen and laugh.
After supper we all
play a trivia game,
and once I even win.

FORGIVENESS

I start walking home from school.
When I hear my name called, I turn around.
It's him; yes, *him*, the one who once asked me,
"Why you do always try to act like one of us?"
All because I earn my A+ report card,
pushing through homework instead of
playing video games, not saying, "You ain't,"
or "You is," or "I'm doing good."
"Hey, man," he says, "I'm sorry for what I said to
you a while back." I freeze in shock before matching
his extended hand with my own. "Wow, thanks, man."
I say. "That means a lot. I'm curious though,
what made you apologize to me?" "Well," he says,
"Last week a couple of African Americans
asked me the same question I asked you."

Apology

When Shonda
presents
her family tree
to the class,

I see all
the top branches
are draped
in chains.

*Because my
ancestors
were slaves,*
she says.

I swallow.
I want to say
I'm
            sorry,
but those words
are so small
for something
so big.

Still I want to try.

So I write it
on a scrap of paper,
find her library book,
and tuck it inside.

OFFICER BRASSARD

When I watch the news, I can't believe when I see people who
could pass as my family being choked, pummeled, shot, *killed*
by police officers. I remember the time when I tried to hop a chain-link
fence, my low-top sneakers got caught, and I couldn't get down.
That's when Officer Brassard happened to drive by. He stopped,
helped me untwist myself, and promised to keep that embarrassing
moment to himself. He even bought me a Popsicle later that day
to help me cool off my shame, a gift for being awesome, he said.
Yet, when the police officers on TV are pale as a cloud,
just like Officer Brassard, it makes my heart twist
without any hope of being disentangled.

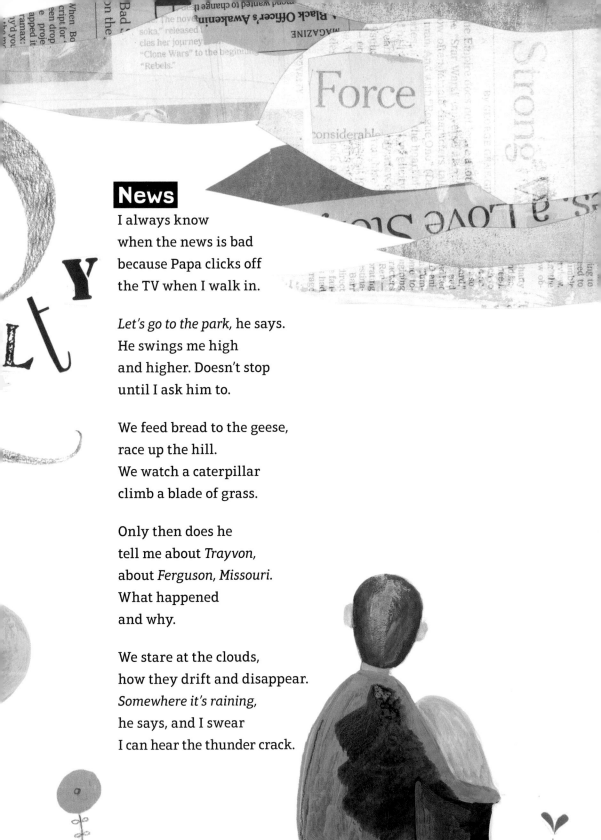

News

I always know
when the news is bad
because Papa clicks off
the TV when I walk in.

Let's go to the park, he says.
He swings me high
and higher. Doesn't stop
until I ask him to.

We feed bread to the geese,
race up the hill.
We watch a caterpillar
climb a blade of grass.

Only then does he
tell me about *Trayvon,*
about *Ferguson, Missouri.*
What happened
and why.

We stare at the clouds,
how they drift and disappear.
Somewhere it's raining,
he says, and I swear
I can hear the thunder crack.

PUNISHMENT

I stare at the ceiling in my bedroom, wondering
why I had to back talk to Mom when she
asked me to do the dishes, and I yelled,
"Why don't you leave me alone?"
It escaped my lips before I could catch it,
now I can't meet Irene at the library after school.
"I can handle a lot of things." Mom said.
"But the one thing me and your father will
never put up with is you being disrespectful."
Then Mom says the dreaded words
no kid should ever have to hear . . .
"Wait till your father gets home."

Punishment

When my brothers
take the box of kitchen matches
and set fire
to a shoebox of old papers,
Mama pulls the paddle
from the top of the fridge
and hands it to Papa
while I hide behind the door.

Later, when I snag a french fry
from off Papa's supper plate,
that fire still blazes
in his eyes
as he pops my hand.
Don't you children
understand
what respect means?

SLEEPOVER

I want to go to my cousin Ronnie's sleepover tonight,
so I ask Mom and Dad. "No can do, kiddo,"
Dad says. "That's a rough neighborhood,
especially in the evening."
"But, Dad," I say, "I hang out there
after school at least once a week."
"Baby, that's during the day," Mom says.
"Why didn't anyone ever tell me this before?" I ask.
"Because sometimes in life," Mom says,
"There are things you aren't supposed
to know until it's necessary."

Why Aunt Sarah Doesn't Go Downtown after Dark

sky
black

streets
black

faces
black

fear
white

THE N-BOMB

Mom, holding my folded laundry, passes
as I'm *nodding, swaying, flowing* into rhythms
that make me start sliding my feet from side to side.
The rapper then punches out a word that makes
her do a double take. "Did he just drop the N-bomb?"
she asks. "Yes," I say. "But it had an *A* at the end of it,
not an *E-R*, so it's okay." "No, it's not," she says, "No matter
how you spell it, it's still a spit in the face of our ancestors,
who for far too long fought against the infection of that word."
"Sorry," I say, pressing the Stop button, not knowing what kind
of music I can listen to anymore that will make me happy.

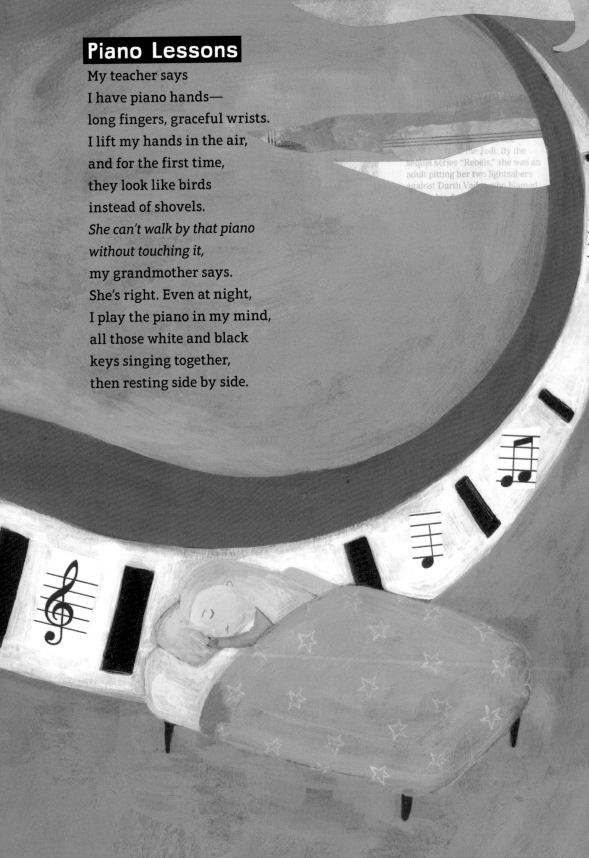

Piano Lessons

My teacher says
I have piano hands—
long fingers, graceful wrists.
I lift my hands in the air,
and for the first time,
they look like birds
instead of shovels.
She can't walk by that piano
without touching it,
my grandmother says.
She's right. Even at night,
I play the piano in my mind,
all those white and black
keys singing together,
then resting side by side.

Bedtime Reading

After homework
I read *The Black Stallion*
for the third time.

I imagine I'm Alec,
coaxing that horse
with seaweed,

and it's me
the stallion is saving
when he stomps
out the snake.

When I find
a note from Shonda
tucked inside the pages,
I can't wait to tell Charles.

*Sorry for freezing you
out of freeze dance*, it says.

I smile
the same way Alec does
when the stallion
nuzzles him
for the very first time.

AUTHOR VISIT

Irene and I stand in line, cradling our books like
newborn kittens. We can't stop smiling.
We're about to meet an author, her name is Nikki Grimes.
We both love her book about kids in someplace called
the Bronx going through life's ups and downs, like us.
I tell Irene that with her beaded earrings, twisty curls, and full lips,
Ms. Grimes is a mirror image of my Auntie Jackie. Irene whispers
when she grows up, she's going to be a writer, go to schools, and sign books.
Mrs. Vandenberg says, "Ms. Grimes, I'd like you to meet
two of your biggest fans," and our faces briefly turn crimson.
Her bracelets jangle as she shakes our hands, takes our books,
then dashes off her name in perfect cursive.
Skipping back to class, Irene and I high-five each other
while our classmates stare at us like we're Martians.

Quiet Time

For the first time ever,
I take a seat beside Charles.
Patty Jean looks at me.
Are you sure?

I'm sure, I say.
Patty Jean shrugs,
takes off her backpack,
sits on my other side.

I tell Charles about
a book I'm reading,
and he doesn't interrupt me
once.

Hey, Charles, I say,
thinking how much
I like being sandwiched
between two friends.

*Show Patty Jean
what Nikki Grimes
wrote inside your book.*

And he does.

BLOOMING FLOWER

I'm sitting next to Irene in class, and everyone is working on the poem project.
It's as quiet as a rock except for the constant shushing being
sent in our direction. Classmates are staring, giving us the evil eye,
it's not helping, shutting up is not an option until Mrs. Vandenberg
walks over and says, "Irene, I never thought I'd ever say this to you,
but you need to be quiet."

Dear Mrs. Vandenberg

Here we are, still getting used to each other, our sideways glances
turning in to high-fives and hanging out together during quiet time.

We smile when we learn we both like books, but not sports.
We nod our heads over cool shoes and colorful laces.

Now we see each other as individuals—vegans, horseback riders, readers.
We share hurts like being left out at recess and getting into trouble with our parents.

Sometimes we say the wrong thing, sometimes we misunderstand.
Now we listen, we ask questions. We are so much more than black and white!

Irene   CHARLES

P.S. Hey, Mrs. Vandenberg, what's our next writing project going to be?

AUTHORS' NOTE

You could say this project began with an e-mail in which one poet (Irene) asked another poet (Charles) to be a writing partner in a conversation about race, about how our individual experiences have shaped our lives. But that explanation doesn't account for the conversations that came before that e-mail—or the books, the questions, the childhoods, and all that happened in the years before we were even born. Specifically, this book would not have happened if not for an inspired and inspiring conversation with our editor Carol Hinz. (Thank you, Carol!) A conversation about race and how we relate to one another is never limited to just that moment but must encompass all that came before—as well as our hopes for the future.

The poems in this collection went through different permutations before we decided to write about what it would be like if we had met in a current-day fifth-grade classroom in a suburban school with a 60 percent white and 40 percent minority population.

In real life, Irene attended fifth grade at Folsom Elementary in Folsom, Louisiana. Charles attended fifth grade at Penrose Elementary in Philadelphia, Pennsylvania. We became acquainted online in 2012 through Poetry Friday and other activities hosted by the children's poetry community. We have yet to meet in person. Our correspondence has been mainly through e-mail and text messaging, with the occasional phone call. It wasn't until we embarked upon the journey of writing this book that we truly became friends.

Fun fact: The teacher in the book, Mrs. Vandenberg, is based on Charles's former teacher, Becky Vandenberg, who has been a beacon of light, not only for Charles but for many of the students she has taught and mentored at Penn Wood High School in Lansdowne, Pennsylvania, since 1988.

While we invented many details to better serve the book, the spirit of each poem is based on our real-life experiences growing up in the 1980s and attending city and suburban public schools. Whether real or imagined, the poems reflect our truest and most honest emotions and recollections about our experiences related to race. Like the speakers in this book, during this poetry project, we experienced fear, but we were open; we made missteps, yet we stumbled forward; and we learned things, and it changed us.

We hope you will find the courage in these pages to have your own conversations about race.

Irene & Charles

ILLUSTRATORS' NOTE

When we first read the manuscript for *Can I Touch Your Hair? Poems of Race, Mistakes, and Friendship*, we liked that the poems were a dialogue between an African American boy and a Caucasian girl—just like us. Right away, we could imagine ourselves in our own childhood classrooms, asking some of the same questions and having many of the same complicated feelings. Both separately and together, we revisited some of the hurts, alienations, curiosities, and hopes we remember feeling as children.

At home—and in our work—we strive to ask each other questions as a way to try to understand each other's points of view. It is a constant process of discovery and learning—one that began eighteen years ago when we first met and continues today through the process of working on art for picture books.

Our illustrations are made using acrylic paint, colored pencil, and collage. Mixing together materials mirrors our philosophy of mixing together our cultures. Our own children are a mix of both of us—and just as we teach them empathy and curiosity at home, we attempt to teach empathy and curiosity to children everywhere through the art in our books.

We hope that this book may ignite conversations about race and identity—conversations that aren't so easy to have but are necessary to gain greater understanding.

Sean & Selina

For Mama, who said, *err on the side of love*,
and for Charles, who said *yes*
—I.L.

For my parents.
For *Poetry Alive!*
For Bob, Rodney, Jennifer, Allan, Kenadine,
John, Camille, Alan, Anita, and Carl.
—C.W.

For the kids at PS 10 in Brooklyn
—S.Q.

For my dear friend Jessica
—S.A.

Carolrhoda Books
A division of Lerner Publishing Group, Inc.
241 First Avenue North
Minneapolis, MN 55401 USA

For reading levels and more information, look up this title at www.lernerbooks.com.

Designed by Danielle Carnito.
Main body text set in Aptifer Slab LT Pro Medium 11/16.5 and Helvetica Neue Light 11/17.5.
Typefaces provided by Linotype AG.
The illustrations in this book were created with acrylic paint, colored pencil, and collage.

Library of Congress Cataloging-in-Publication Data

Names: Latham, Irene, author. | Waters, Charles, 1973– author. | Qualls, Sean, illustrator. | Alko, Selina, illustrator.
Title: Can I touch your hair? : poems of race, mistakes, and friendship / by Irene Latham and Charles Waters ; Illustrators: Sean Qualls and Selina Alko.
Description: Minneapolis : Carolrhoda Books, 2018.
Identifiers: LCCN 2017006279 (print) | LCCN 2016045348 (ebook) | ISBN 9781512404425 (lb : alk. paper) | ISBN 9781512408881 (eb pdf)
Subjects: LCSH: Race awareness—Juvenile poetry. | Race relations—Juvenile poetry. | Friendship—Juvenile poetry.
Classification: LCC PS3612.A8685 C36 2018 (ebook) | LCC PS3612.A8685 (print) | DDC 811/.6—dc23

LC record available at https://lccn.loc.gov/2017006279

Manufactured in the United States of America
1-39213-21106-5/16/2017